Numerology

Numerology for beginners, and how to use numerology and numbers for success in your relationships, career, dreams, and goals!

Table of Contents

Introduction iv

Chapter 1. The Meanings and Energies behind Numbers... 1

Chapter 2. Using Numerology to Decode Yourself and Other People 8

Chapter 3. Using Numerology to Understand Past, Present, and Future 27

Chapter 4. Using Numerology to Develop Your Psychic Powers 30

Conclusion.. 34

Introduction

I want to thank you and congratulate you for downloading the book, *"Numerology"*.

This book contains helpful information about numerology, what it is, and how to use it. You will learn about the history of numerology, and why it has lasted so long in many different cultures.

You will learn the meanings of different numbers, and be able to calculate the numbers that correspond with your name, birthday, the year, and month.

With the help of this book, you'll be able to understand how your name and birth date affect your personality, strengths, weaknesses, trials and tribulations, and to some extent your destiny. Having this knowledge will allow you to improve your weaknesses, and move in a positive direction with your life.

You will also learn about using numerology to improve your psychic abilities. Numerology can be associated with both ESP and divination, and can help you to improve both of these skills.

This book will explain to you tips and techniques that will allow you to easily begin using the power of numerology to enhance your life, starting today!

Thanks again for downloading this book, I hope you enjoy it!

Chapter 1. The Meanings and Energies behind Numbers

Numerology is a two thousand year old practice of deciphering the patterns that underlie people's characters and destinies in life by analyzing numbers. Pythagoras, the Greek philosopher, is considered as one of the proponents of numerology because of his belief that everything is governed by energies that are represented by numbers. As the centuries passed, people picked up on Pythagoras' teachings and contributed to his material. Other cultures such as the Hebrews, the Hindus, the Chinese, the Arabs, and the Egyptians also have their own numerological systems. Thus, the various forms of numerology are collaborations of several minds that are fascinated by math and metaphysics.

Even though numerology has gone through two millennia (and possibly longer than that), it has persisted up to the present. This means that countless of people all over the world have found the practice useful and insightful, so they have passed it on to the next generations. Now, it's your turn to learn this timeless art of glimpsing the energetic currents that shape the universe.

According to numerologists, dates and letters give a set of energies to individuals, objects, and events. These dictate how they become. There are those who say that people acquire their birthdays and names in accordance to a divine plan. Whether you believe in predestination or not, you will gain a lot of insight from numerological analysis.

These are some of the things that you will be able to do when you study numerology:

- Understand yourself more
- Know your strengths and weaknesses
- Find your place in life
- Gain insights about other people's natures and paths
- Comprehend why you encountered certain experiences
- Predict what will happen on future dates
- Perceive energies behind ideas, places, objects, etc.
- Strengthen your psychic abilities

Excited yet? Before anything else, you need to familiarize yourself with what numbers mean.

Number Meanings

In numerology, the numbers one to nine are associated with certain ideas and traits. Spend some time to reflect on each number – this will make it easier for you to make evaluations later on.

- One

Number 1 begins all the other numbers. Its energy translates to beginnings, individuality, and leadership. It is dominant and aggressive. People with the frequency of number 1 are leaders, organizers, planners, and pioneers. They often create original things and pave new paths. They strive to be on top. Their strong personalities enable them to overcome trials in life and inspire others to do the same. Being highly individualistic, they have their personal convictions and they don't subscribe to an idea or tradition just because it's popular. Arrogance and selfishness are two negative traits of this number. To make you understand this number better, think of it as Yang energy. It is masculine, forceful, and self-directed.

- Two

1 and 1 put together makes 2, thus this number contains the energy of attraction and partnership. Number 2 is all

about union, balance and harmony. While number 1 is masculine, number 2 is feminine; characteristics that are traditionally ascribed to women are also linked to this number – gentleness, passiveness, and compassion. People having this number are kind and cooperative. They are also emotional, sensitive, and artistic. If number 2 individuals are not careful, they may have problems in controlling their emotions and making decisions. This number represents Yin energy because it is feminine, receptive, and dependent.

- Three

Communication, expression, and interaction are attributed to number 3. It is assigned those meanings because it is the number that follows the calm and silent number 2. Number 3 people are cheerful and energetic. They are popular, charming, and sociable. They are highly intelligent and can learn many things at the same time. They are good communicators and can express themselves in a lot of ways such as through singing, writing, and more. The bad sides of number 3 can cause a person to be prone to exaggerations and foolish behavior. Number 3 can be thought of as a burst of expansive energy or a child that was born from the union of 2.

- Four

Number 4 is a solid and secure number. It brings an earthy energy that's manifested by practicality, determination, and tradition. Number 4 individuals are patient, hardworking, and faithful. They are motivated to build and maintain things. Their cautiousness makes them refrain from breaking rules and taking chances impulsively. Like number one characters, number fours are strong-willed and they tend to lead instead of follow. The bad side of number four is that it can cause people to become stubborn and restrictive. Remember what number 4 means by imagining it as a square or a home with four sides.

- Five

The fifth number is linked with the 5 senses. It also stands for change and movement because it's one step ahead of the stable number 4. Its energy is versatile, mobile, and curious. Number 5 people are risk takers and investigators. They love freedom and variety. They are smart and sociable like number 3 individuals, but they also like traveling. The negative aspect of number 5 can drive individuals to trickery, restlessness, and overindulgence.

Picture a five point star in a wheel to remember what number 5 means.

- Six

The number 6 harbors the energy of a caretaker. Coming after sensual number 5, number 6 is loving, responsible and self-sacrificing. Number 6 folks love to help others. They strive to maintain harmony and fairness, may it be in the home, in their relationships, and in the things they are interested in. They can give good advice to others who seek their counsel. If you have this energy, avoid sacrificing too much at the expense of your own welfare. You can relate number 6 to a responsible and caring mother.

- Seven

Number 7 enters the scene after 6 takes care of matters. It's about resting and turning inward. People with 7 energy are thinkers, philosophers, and seers who are in tune with intellectual and spiritual affairs. They are seekers of wisdom, which they attain through research, analysis, and meditation. The negative side of 7 causes illusions, aloofness, and impracticality. The 7 colors of the rainbow is a visual reminder of what the number signifies – it illuminates people and links land (matter) and sky (spirit) together.

- Eight

Number 8 is the testing ground for the insights gained by number 7. The previous number is concerned with inner power – this number is all about outer power. It speaks of authority and achievement. It processes number 7 ideals into tangible reality. Individuals with number 8 energy are successful, efficient, and decisive. On the downside, they can be controlling, insensitive, and brutal. The infinity symbol is similar to the number 8 – this will prompt you to recall its powerful nature.

- Nine

The number 9 signifies completion and release. After 8 has implemented things that needed to be done, 9 takes over to finalize things. Because it also symbolizes the whole, it brings a global perspective to those who carry its energy. 9 individuals are humanitarians and visionaries. They always have the big picture in mind. They think outside of the box and they are also highly intuitive. Nine may cause aimlessness and laziness, though. After 9 months, the pregnancy ends and a baby is born – leading back to number 1.

Chapter 2. Using Numerology to Decode Yourself and Other People

Finding the Numerical Equivalent of Names and Birthdays

Words and names can be studied through numerology by converting each of their letters into numbers.

1 – A, J, S
2 – B, K, T
3 – C, L, U
4 – D, M, V
5 – E, N, W
6 – F, O, X
7 – G, P, Y
8 – H, Q, Z
9 – I, R

Special Characters

If your name has unique letters like Ñ, you may use the alphabet that contains the character. Ñ is present in the Spanish alphabet. You can get its numerology value by ordering the Spanish letters and arranging them into 9 rows. Otherwise, use the letter that is most similar to it (ex. N for Ñ)

Spanish Alphabet

1 – A, I, Q, Z
2 – B, J, R
3 – C, L, RR
4 – CH, LL, S
5 – D, M, T
6 – E, N, U
7 – F, Ñ, V
8 – G, O, X
9 – H, P, Y

If your name originates from a particular language that has a different set of letters than the English alphabet, list the alphabet for that language and assign numbers to them like what was done above.

Name Analysis

Personality number – This represents your outward aspects and affects your impression on other people. To calculate this, add the numerical equivalents of the *consonants* (B, C, D, F, G, H, J, K, L, M, N, P, Q, R, S, T, V, W, X, Y, Z) in the name and reduce the sum into a number between 1 to 9.

Inner Urge number – This symbolizes your inner temperament and your deepest motivations. You get this number by adding the numerical equivalents of the *vowels* (A, E, I, O, U) in the name and reducing it into a number between 1 to 9.

Expression number – This signifies the totality of your being. The expression number is computed through adding the numerical equivalents of the *consonants and vowels* in the name and reducing the result into a number between 1 to 9.

In-depth Name Analysis

Aside from getting the overall personality quality, you can also find the specific traits that you are blessed with and those that you lack. To find out your strengths and weaknesses, get the number equivalent of each letter of your name. Tally the number of times that a digit appears.

For example:

K E A N U C H A R L E S R E E V E S

2, 5, 1, 5, 3, .3, 8, 1, 9, 3, 5, 1, 9, 5, 5, 4, 5, 1

1: 4

2: 1

3: 3

4: 1

5: 6

6: 0

7: 0

8: 1

9: 2

5 predominates Keanu Reeves' name, thus giving him an intensely intellectual nature. He lacks 6 and 7 – the numbers for harmony and introspection. This may mean that although he thinks about things a lot, he has an inner turmoil that he refuses to acknowledge. This is a reasonable guess since he has experienced a lot of heartaches in his life, such as his troubled childhood and the untimely death of his wife and daughter. His next most common number, 1, supports his tendency to be reserved about his feelings (number 2).

Strengths

If the name contains a lot of the following numbers, the person may have these strengths:

1: leadership qualities, independence, motivation, originality
2: sensitivity, diplomacy, cooperation, humility
3: optimism, good communication skills, sociability, wit
4: practicality, reliability, attention to detail, discipline
5: versatility, resourcefulness, intelligence, free spirit
6: artistic skills, even temperament, responsibility, service-oriented
7: analytical abilities, wisdom, introspective tendencies
8: ambition, drive for success, managerial abilities
9: compassion, humanitarianism, tolerance

Weaknesses

If the name lacks these numbers or has very few of them, the person may have weaknesses such as the following:

1: absence of motivation, dependence on others, cowardice
2: rebelliousness, insensitivity, tactless, withheld emotions
3: pessimism, difficulty in expression, dullness
4: unreliability, impracticality, carelessness, lack of self-control
5: stubbornness, fear of change and new experiences
6: irresponsibility, lack of concern for others
7: a dislike of analysis, shallow mindedness

8: can't handle money well, lacks authority, not good in decision making

9: narrow mindedness, being cold hearted, selfishness

Birthday Analysis

Aside from names, birthdays also matter a lot in numerology.

Birth Path number – This gives an insight to the general characteristics of his/her life. This is calculated by adding the numbers in the full birth date and reducing it into a number between 1 to 9.

Jan - 1
Feb - 2
March - 3
April - 4
May - 5
June - 6
July - 7
August - 8
September - 9
October – 10/1
November – 11/2
December – 12/3

Let's use these dates as examples:

January 17, 1967

1+1+7+1+9+6+7 = 32 = 3+2 = 5

The birth path number of this person is described by the number 5 (variety, freedom). This point out to a life that offers him varied experiences and a chance to find his ultimate freedom.

December 7, 1985

12+7+1+9+8+5 = 42 = 4+2 = 6

This describes a life geared towards harmony and responsibility. This individual is likely to be a peacemaker who is interested in helping others.

Birth Path

If you have the number _ as your birth path, numerology tells that you live:

1 – To start something, to lead others, to be the best in a particular field
2 – To work with others, to understand people, to restore balance

3 – To express yourself, to inspire others, to cultivate friendships

4 – To work hard, to be stable, to be reliable, to provide security

5 – To experience life, to travel, to achieve freedom, to adapt to changes

6 – To be responsible, to care, to bring beauty and harmony

7 – To find wisdom, to know the truth, to teach others

8 – To achieve success, to wield money and power, to make wise decisions

9 – To widen horizons, to be compassionate, to serve humanity.

Birthday Number – The day of birth contributes to the energy of the birth path. It provides more information about what you are born with and what you can expect from your life.

1 – Those born on the first day of the month have strong number 1 energy in their personality makeup. They have a lot of drive and can be impatient and domineering at times.

2 – Being born on the second day gives a tendency to be more emotional and sensitive than most people. Those

born on this day need to be careful of losing their identity when dealing with others deeply.

3 – A birthday on the third day of the month bestows cheerfulness and resiliency. However, since the number 3 energy is undiluted, those born on the third of the month should guard against its negative traits such as lack of focus and naivety.

4 – With a birthday on the fourth day comes a natural skill to be practical and disciplined. Those born on this day must avoid being too harsh on themselves and others, though.

5 – Being born on the fifth day makes people crave travel and varied experiences. It might be challenging for them to settle down.

6 – A birthday on this day nurtures an extra caring personality. The advice for Day 6 birthday celebrants is to avoid spreading themselves too thinly and save some love for themselves.

7 – Those born on this day are introverts who prefer deep thought over trivial preoccupations. They tend to pursue the mystical arts, including numerology. They should

strive to balance their lofty pursuits with fulfilling the obligations of everyday life.

8 – People with birthdays on the eighth day are business-minded and good leaders. They can achieve great success – but only if they work really hard for it.

9 – Having a birthday on the ninth day can result into a drive to be merciful to others because of an immensely broad perspective. This is learned through challenging life experiences that improve the person's character.

10 – Number 10 is 1 times 10, so those born on the tenth of the month can have an amazing amount of yang energy. They must use their powers wisely and avoid aggravating the flaws of this number.

11 – Number 11 is considered as a master number in some numerology traditions. Since 11 is associated with spirituality, those born on the eleventh tend to become mystics. Also, since 11 can be reduced to 2, they're very sensitive to the point that they seem like they have psychic powers. However, those with this number can become ungrounded if they're not careful.

12 – This number is composed of numbers 1 and 2 and thus it partially contains the energies of both numbers plus

the resultant number 3. This gives those born on the twelfth a balance of individuality and agreeableness, which make them popular among diverse groups. On the downside, they tend to have a dual personality, thus they need to be clear on what's really important for them.

13 – Those born on the thirteenth are excellent workers – focused, driven, intelligent, and patient. Their combined powers of one and three are translated into reliable results. Because they are well rewarded in their pursuits, they tend to become workaholics, which may deplete their energy.

14 – The overall energy of those born on the fourteenth is found in number 5, thus they are versatile, intelligent, and skilled conversationalists. They may also be good leaders and reliable workers. They may lack warmth and cheerfulness though – if they work on these, they'll become more charismatic.

15 – Those born on day 15 of the month gravitate to service because they find it reasonable to help those in need. They are pioneers and revolutionaries who aim to improve the condition of humanity. This might give them a rather stressful and lonely existence. They will live fulfilling lives if they also find some joy for themselves instead of just making the rest of the world happy.

16 – Individuals born on the sixteenth day are motivated to seek knowledge to help themselves and other people. They can be quite charismatic and attract people's attention, yet they prefer to be alone. They can be perfectionists at times.

17 – Numbers one and seven work together to create a mind that's original and imaginative. People born on the seventeenth are inventors and geniuses who can translate their insights into tangible things. They can achieve fame because of their talents, yet they can sometimes feel undeserving of recognition.

18 – Those born on day 18 are achievers in many areas. They have a keen understanding of many things, including human nature. Because of this, they can become advisors. Their high status can make them intolerant of flaws, however.

19 – Because 19 has energies of both 1 and 9, people born on the 19th are prone to initiate actions and bring them into completion. They are similar to those born on day 5 because they frequently go through various phases. Their abundant energy can lead them to extremes so they need to develop the balance of number 2.

20 – Since 20 is ten times 2, people born on the twentieth have magnified number two energy. They are extremely cooperative and sensitive, which draws people towards them. This should not make them abandon their wellbeing for the sake of pleasing others.

21 – People with a birth day that results in the number 3 are highly sociable. If they are born on the 21st, they are genuinely interested in other people instead of simply enjoying themselves. They prefer to keep things simple, which may prevent them from making deep conversation.

22 – The number 22 is considered by some as a master number which stands for supreme builder. They crave order above all so they are meticulous and controlling with everything. This may conflict with their doubled need to be accepted by other people.

23 – Numbers 2 and 3 make people born on the 23rd day become adept with using words to influence others. They can be prominent entertainers and persuaders but their changeable nature may lead others to distrust them.

24 – People born on the twenty-fourth day of the month care for other people and work hard to assist them. When they decide to put their efforts to something, they do so out

of sincere dedication. They can be restrictive at times, so they must learn to give room for those they love.

25 – Those born on day 25 of the month are prolific thinkers. They ponder a lot before they act. Although they are smarter than most people, they can miss opportunities because of their indecisiveness.

26 – People born on the twenty-sixth are ambitious yet they try not to trample on others as they climb to the top. They can be successful in both charity work and business affairs. They are generous individuals who don't hesitate to lend others a hand, which may cause them to be taken advantage of.

27 – Those born on the 27th have a lot of interests, but they usually have something to do with higher thought such as psychology, philosophy, spirituality, and the occult. They accumulate knowledge from various sources, which they can teach to others in order to help them with their problems.

28 – Individuals born on day 28 of the month are leaders who connect well with the people they lead. Their pioneering and organizational skills work wonderfully in everything they do. Because they can be too focused on

accomplishing things, they might neglect to simply feel and be.

29 – 2 and 9 adds up to 11, which is the master number for illumination. Thus, those born on the 29 may be considered as illuminated because they acquire a lot of wisdom. They tend to find themselves in large groups of people who work for a common cause. This may cause them to feel superior, which they should avoid if they want to be of genuine service to mankind.

30 – Those born on the thirtieth day have powerful number three energy in their system. They can be inspirers and leaders among their social circles. They should use their talents of speech to accomplish worthwhile things instead of simply generating gossip.

31 – People born on the thirty-first day of the month are reliable communicators who have high ideals. They can be trusted to work on a goal with mental focus and intelligence. Because they can be very intellectual, they might neglect feelings (their own and those of others) for the sake of order and goal achievement.

Maturity Number – This tells you what you are aiming for in life. As the sum of the expression number (consonants and vowels of name) and birth path number (birthday), this is the interplay of who you are and where you're headed. It's called as 'maturity number' because it only activates when you hit your thirties.

Career

There are certain professions that fit people with a dominant number type.

1. Inventor, engineer, politician, designer, entrepreneur
2. Diplomat, health care provider, minister, artist, teacher, advisor
3. Teacher, writer, performer, entertainer, salesperson, cheerleader, coach
4. Banker, organizer, engineer, builder, craftsman, doctor, surgeon
5. Businessman, advertiser, salesman, entertainer
6. Health care provider, restaurant or hotel owner, teacher, welfare work, decorator, therapist
7. Philosopher, researcher, detective, teacher, psychic, programmer, specialist
8. Leader, CEO, supervisor, manager, government official, administrator

9. Psychologist, artist, orator, lawyer, judge, artist, health professional, healer, humanitarian

The occupations above are only suggestions based on the general characteristics of each number. Each person has about 5 important numbers – these and other factors will influence what job he/she will choose and excel at.

Love

This is brief portrait of how people having a certain number type behave when they're in love:

1. Individualistic; can take a dominant role in a relationship
2. A pleaser; will sacrifice for the sake of the partner
3. Very expressive and entertaining; will use his/her creativity to spice things up
4. Will try to discipline from his/her significant other, works hard for both
5. Will prize his/her freedom and yearn for varied experiences
6. A responsible lover who will help his/her partner
7. Very introspective; considers the relationship as a learning experience
8. Concentrates on accomplishments

9. Compassionate and tolerant

As with the previous list, a person can display traits from different numbers. Check his/her complete numerological profile (birth path number, personality number, inner urge number, expression number, etc.) to know what to expect.

Relationships among the Numbers

Make a detailed number analysis for your partner or potential mate. Then, compare each of his/her numbers with yours. If the difference between your number and the other person is:

1. You must let your partner be him or herself.
2. You need to be more sensitive to the other person.
3. Communication is important in the relationship.
4. Set reasonable limits and do your best.
5. Do not restrict your partner's freedom.
6. You have to harmonize aspects of the relationship.
7. Expect plenty of introspection and truth-seeking when you're together.
8. Beware of power plays; let love guide your interactions.

The kind of numbers you use will tell you where to apply the instructions above. For example, if you used the inner urge numbers and got the difference of 3, it means that you both need frequent talks with each other. If you based your computations on the birth path numbers and got the number 7, your experiences as a couple will be insightful.

Chapter 3. Using Numerology to Understand Past, Present, and Future

Do these to make calculations simpler:

- Know your birth path number (see the previous chapter)
- Simplify the numbers of your birth date into a single digit (month, day, year)

Pinnacles

There are periods of your life that are ruled by specific number energies – the pinnacle number and the challenge number. The pinnacle is called as such because it is the energy that supports you so that you reach your peak. The time periods for each pinnacle are as follows:

- First pinnacle – Subtract your birth path number from 36. If you have 6 as your birth path number, your first pinnacle is 30 years long (36-6).
- Second pinnacle – Starts from the end of the first pinnacle and lasts 9 years.
- Third pinnacle – Starts from the end of the second pinnacle and lasts 9 years.

- Fourth pinnacle – Starts from the end of the third pinnacle and lasts for the remainder of life.

To know the dominant number for each pinnacle, perform the following computations:

- First pinnacle number: month + day
- Second pinnacle number: day + year
- Third pinnacle number: first pinnacle number + second pinnacle number
- Fourth pinnacle number: month + year

Challenges

Challenges are trials that you have to overcome in order to evolve. Each challenge period lasts as long as its corresponding pinnacle period. These are the computations for challenge numbers:

- First challenge number: the difference between day and month of birth
- Second challenge number: the difference between year and day of birth
- Third challenge number: the difference between the first and second challenge numbers
- Fourth challenge number: the difference between the year and month of birth

Reduce the sums and differences into single numbers. By knowing the number for each pinnacle and challenge period, you will comprehend your past and present experiences and you can prepare for what may likely happen in the future.

If you got a 0 for a challenge number, it means that you can choose to have all or none of the challenges that each number represents. Perhaps you have already learned your lessons in previous lives. Congratulations!

Personal Year

Aside from the major time periods, you can also know the 'flavor' of specific years. Add your birth month number, birth day, and the calendar year, and then reduce the sum to one digit.

Personal Month

Each month of every year also has its own energy. Know the personal month number by adding the month number and the personal year number, then reducing the sum into a single number.

Chapter 4. Using Numerology to Develop Your Psychic Powers

ESP (extra-sensory perception) is an ability that is present in all individuals, but there are some people who are more in tune with it than others. Numerology can help develop this skill in you. By familiarizing yourself with the energies of numbers, you will also learn how to perceive energies around you. This makes you aware of more things than what you get from your ordinary senses.

The most important thing in practicing ESP is clearing the mind. Our awareness is flooded with our thoughts and perceptions. Because of this, it's hard to detect faint signals within and around us. By removing as much distractions as we possibly can, we can perceive more things than what we are used to. This is why psychics and mediums go into a trance – this allows them to get in touch with non-physical realities that are as real as the ordinary reality that we are most familiar with.

You can achieve a psychic trance by calming down your body, emotions, and mind. Begin by fully relaxing your body. Loosen tight muscles and be in a position that is most comfortable for you. Breathe slowly, savoring every breath. Let go of your concerns for a while. Imagine your thoughts and feelings as clouds that fly above you – they are gradually getting smaller until they fade into the horizon. If you want, you can also count from 9 to 1, with each count bringing you deeper and deeper into a trance.

You will soon notice that it's hard to focus and images will appear in your mind. This state is similar to what you experience between sleeping and waking up. Do not allow yourself to fall asleep at this point. Stay awake by focusing on one thing such as a mantra, an affirmation, or a symbol such as a number or series of numbers.

When you have regained a focused yet relaxed awareness, you can now perceive freely or concentrate on a subject or a question. You will receive responses in the form of visuals, sounds, and other kinds of insights. If you are highly familiar with number energies at this point, the answers will come in number format. As an example, you might wonder how the next day will be like. In reply, your mind creates a picture of the number 1. This gives you an idea that you will do something new tomorrow. Another example: you want to know how your relationship with a person you just met will turn out. You might hear the band name, "Five for Fighting." This tells you a lot: five means changes and unpredictability, while fighting literally means conflict. You then prepare yourself for possible disagreements with the person.

Remember: this will work only if you have understood the numbers deeply enough that your subconscious mind assimilates the meanings within itself. You have to meditate on each number regularly until your psychic mind can recognize the energies and translate it into numbers. That way, you will understand what your ESP picks up.

Another way to use numerology for divination is to randomly pick a group of numbers and convert the sum of all those into a single digit. For example: if you want to know the end result of a particular project you're working on, concentrate on the topic and then write down the numbers that pop in your head; let's use 16, 2, 9, 28, and 55. Do it quickly so you have no time to calculate a desired number. Adding them together gives you 110 or 2. This tells you that your project will result into a balance of some sort. This is understandable if it deals with balancing your budget, but if it's a competition, it might result in an unexpected tie.

Conclusion

Thank you again for downloading this book!

I hope this book was able to help you learn more about numerology!

The next step is to put this information to use, and begin using the power of numerology to enhance your life!

Finally, if you enjoyed this book, please take the time to share your thoughts and post a review on Amazon. It'd be greatly appreciated!

Thank you and good luck!

www.ingramcontent.com/pod-product-compliance
Lightning Source LLC
LaVergne TN
LVHW021743060526
838200LV00052B/3438